WHERE WE LIVE

THE HUGH MACLENNAN POETRY SERIES

Editors: Allan Hepburn and Carolyn Smart

TITLES IN THE SERIES

Where We Live

John Reibetanz

McGill-Queen's University Press
Montreal & Kingston • London • Chicago

© McGill-Queen's University Press 2016

ISBN 978-0-7735-4676-9 (paper)
ISBN 978-0-7735-9883-6 (ePDF)
ISBN 978-0-7735-9884-3 (ePUB)

Legal deposit first quarter 2016
Bibliothèque nationale du Québec

Printed in Canada on acid-free paper that is 100% ancient forest free (100% post-consumer recycled), processed chlorine free

McGill-Queen's University Press acknowledges the support of the Canada Council for the Arts for our publishing program. We also acknowledge the financial support of the Government of Canada through the Canada Book Fund for our publishing activities.

Library and Archives Canada Cataloguing in Publication

Reibetanz, John, 1944–, author
    Where we live/John Reibetanz.

    (The Hugh MacLennan poetry series)
    Poems.
    Includes bibliographical references.
    Issued in print and electronic formats.
    ISBN 978-0-7735-4676-9 (paperback).
    ISBN 978-0-7735-9883-6 (pdf).
    ISBN 978-0-7735-9884-3 (epub)

    I. Title. II. Series: Hugh MacLennan poetry series

PS8585.E448W44 2016   C811'.54   C2015-906939-4
                                       C2015-906940-8

This book was typeset by Interscript in 9.5/13 New Baskerville.

To Julie,
ζωή μου

CONTENTS

I

THRESHOLDS

THE COILED SHELL

You are at the moon   my son's French teacher used to wail
to his class of mind-wandering nine-year-olds   and though
there were many things he didn't know   such as how to

teach French to Grade Four kids   he had learned that no
   matter
where they seemed to be   they were living elsewhere   rowing
their desks through seas strafed by cannonballs   or launch-
   ing space

probes with freshly sharpened yellow rockets   and Monsieur
sensed that wherever they really lived   someone there had
even before they learned the alphabet   filled their heads

with the hieroglyphics of a foreign language they
alone could decipher   each wrinkle-free brow cloaking
its Rosetta Stone   he may even have suspected

that they held truths as far beyond his reach as the moon
take these three kids who   as they walk along the verge   one
pointing the way   one juggling a ball   one showing off

his muscles   all balance over their heads a snail shell
six times their height   in joyous emulation of   as they
would never tell you   Tecciztecatl   the Aztec

moon god who bore on his back the whorled shell of the
   round
nocturnal creature   whose now-you-see-me now-you-don't
comings and goings mimed the wanderings of that coiled

shell in the night sky   and whose anti-clockwise spiral
repeats the Milky Way's unwinding   informed not with
the lore of clocks or teachers   but of gods and children

GEORGE WASHINGTON CROSSES
THE DELAWARE IN P.S. 140

and I cross it with him crouched in the backwards 7
his leg makes perched on the rowboat's bench   I am 7

too but that *too*'s different from the number 2 Miss Card
has written to show what grade we're in   on the blackboard

that runs beneath the boat and the dark ice-chunked river
my hand can skim if I lower my left arm over

the gunwale   while my right hand rows a pencil spreading
a wake of wavy letters across the page   the rest

of me stowed away with Washington journeying towards
tangled green squiggles his eye lines up on a blue shore

where I stare too until lines on the blackboard break loose
from each other and float   lines gliding like the liners

Miss Card names for us when they pass below our window
each towed by its own puffing tugboats through the Narrows

each with the same first name   Essess Liberté   Essess
United States   the only other boy in my class

called John has a different second name   not Washington
though Miss Card says Washington's son was also called John.

***

The other John never reached the far blue shore   capsized
by a bus on his way home from school   the S.S.s

all turned into scrap or floating gambling palaces
the mural into dust when P.S. 140 was

leveled   but it still hovers in the air of the lost
classroom   and in that space the painter left me to cross

the icy narrows   a pen rows in his brush's wake
and bears me on   founding child of a dream republic

captain and now sole keeper of the painted river
and the school that sailed away with its vanished children.

PHONEBOOTH NOSTALGIA

from the German of Durs Grünbein

Facing the phone once more, on show in the glass
  Box, the door barely closed, a frozen
Han Solo, a tourist attraction for sidewalk passers-
  By, you stare at the small square buttons'
Launchpad, this field of figures dancing like
  Bears in the enchanted forest
Of a night sky ... decimalized mandala flickering,
  Alluring you with pre-Wi-Fi
Sudden nearnesses of whisper, betrayal,
  Even love – life set in ciphers
A long time ago in a far-away galaxy,
  No sooner called up now than – blast-
Off! – a voice rockets your cerebral cortex.

IN MEMORY I LIE

Let's go back to the age of turntables
and seventy-eight rpm records.
My father is listening, over and
over again, to one of his favourites,
Heddle Nash singing *Je crois entendre*,
from Bizet's *Pearl Fishers*: *In memory
I lie beneath the palms and dream of love.*

There are no palms, because the sofa my
father lies on sits in a Brooklyn cold-
water flat. He probably is dreaming
of love because my mother is away,
confined for the past month to the Creedmoor
Psychiatric Center where there are no
palms either, and where dreams of love are made
difficult by electroshock treatments.

Yet there were no palms in the studio
where Nash recorded his song: only *in
memory* did he lie beneath them and
*hear a voice more tender than the fluting
of the dove*, and the sounds my father hears
come from no living voice but from fluting
carved in a wax master by a stylus.

The needle on the turntable only
seems to ride onwards through the record's grooves.
It really sits in one place while the disc
spins round and round, just as the song's "she" *seems
to wander through the trees* but is frozen
in memory, a statue with *mantle
gently glowing*, mute in the singer's mind,
his voice companioned only by static.

Let's use the sound technology of a
later age to fast-forward fifteen years.
Visiting home, waking on the sofa,
I hear their voices in the kitchen, hers
shaky though long calmed, his clear and quibbling:
their bickering, no singing, to my ear
makes, truer than memory, a music.

WHITE AND BLACK

There were few consequences when Buffy staked vampires – they
turned to dust and then disappeared; it was all very black and white.
Real life, of course, isn't so black and white.

Lynne Edwards

Salt   unlike vampires   never savours mortal life   keeps
to himself in an all-white neighbourhood of crystal
coffins   yet never knows death   unlike his underground

cousins   oil and coal   whose blackness is pure extinction
welling from petrified bodies of protoplankton
and who   like us   burn their essence into energy

and leave the spent residue to air and earth   while salt
persists like the ancient gods   surrounded by small lives
and deaths   unkillable   if you drown him he returns

crystal by crystal once water has breathed out its last
as vapour   the pristine grains sliding through your fingers
coolly   neither seeping into pores nor smudging skin

with dust   if you asked Mother Earth which of her children
brought her more pain   black-veined Coal a.k.a. liquid Oil
or white-faced Salt   she would turn her round head
    and   shrugging

show you the holes in her skull   drilled to deliver both
but if you asked my father which was the villain   he
would opt for black   having spent years of hours trying

to scrub away the tarry residue of workdays
at Vulcan Rubber Proofing   yet you cannot ask him
because he's dust now   vanquished by no vampire but by

the hard white rain that sprinkled on his plate   and slower
but more efficient than when poured on open wounds   seeped
into his blood   wrung his heart   and ended his real life.

MURANO GLASS

My father never got to visit Venice   except
through my eyes now   as they drift into the shopwindow
of *Murano Glass* and startle at his middle-aged

face staring out at me   same hairline I remember
though edged with darker fringe   as if the bright glass reversed
aging's direction   same laugh wrinkles   same watery

blue irises   cheeks hazed however   with a ghostly
transparency   that cannot keep shelved amber bottles
so like the labeled ones his live hands loved to reach for

from entering his head while   streaming from his shoulders
currents of Grand Canal   mirrored in plate glass   wrap him
in a cape whose watered silk flows with the filmy sheen

of his passed-down boy scout metal shaving mirror   where
does one life end and another begin   or do they
interpenetrate like these rippling lights   each human

frame built like the white stone palazzo behind our shared
window-image   on a foundation of shimmering
reflections   questions to be pursued when I visit

my son who bears his own name   followed by mine   then by
my father's   and I see myself shining through his glassed
photographs of Venice   steeping in the Grand Canal

MISSED CONNECTION

Delayed that morning, long after she died,
after you'd lived alone in the suddenly large
little house, after you'd been found
wandering the mall lot searching for a car

you'd sold decades ago, I arrived in time
to walk with you in late afternoon around
the home's closed courtyard, and you, your room-
number pinned to your shirt pocket, remembered

how, that morning, walking there, she'd said
the fountain's whisper took her back to the seaside
cottage you'd stayed in on your honeymoon,
where the same rugosas overran the garden.

Had I been with you on that morning stroll,
there would have been three of us listening through the roses.

None left standing   a few last stalwarts nearly upright
lean propped against comrades   unbuttressed they would
   teeter
then topple like felled pillars   the rest bent or bowed
   whipped

headlong earthwards   is it TV's carnage   live nightly
from the fertile crescent   that makes my eye overlay
this harvest-ripe wheatfield with insurrection's twisted

aftermath   or friends' accounts of uprisings put down
when caterpillar tracks blighted Budapest's flagged rows
in '56 or Prague's in '68   or is it

congenital weakness in the nerves passed down from my
own protesting trodden ancestors   an heirloom tic
from 1848 Baden on the father's side

or 1798 Dublin on the mother's
whatever starved ghosts shadow my sight   a fresh look casts
them out   stalk-loops too infused with leap to be a dance

of death   headlong arcs more reel than whiplash   plumped
   tassels
flinging not flung   Brueghel rather than Bosch   it must be
these bending ears have heard they will rise once more
   as bread

Bendt Ahlgreen: the patient ahead of me, name waiting
above mine on the sign-in sheet, even though the name's
bearer had gone shuffling west where I was striding east.

"Bendt" fits a stooped man making his way effortfully
with a cane, but "Ahlgreen?" Pale brown the skin on his
    arms,
wrinkled neck, bald head, brown of withered oak foliage.

Yet I saw only summer's leavings, and maybe like
oak branches in winter, he carried his green inside,
not "all green" but "Ahlgreen"   the "ah" of a green deeply

inhaled, past springs patiently waiting to spring again.

SONNETS TO ORPHEUS, 1:21

from the German of Rainer Maria Rilke

Spring has awakened once more, the Earth's
like a young child who's learned poems by heart –
many, so many ... Now unburdened
of her long lessons, she wins the gold star.

Her teacher was strict, though we loved the snow
in the whiskers of the old man.
Now, when we ask her about the names
of the green and the blue, she knows, she knows!

Earth, on holiday, happily playing
tag with the children, how can we catch you,
overjoyed Earth. The most joyful wins:

what the teacher taught her, the many lectures
printed in roots and in the long
intricate stems, she sings, she sings!

THE BASSWOOD BEDSTEAD

"We are now going," said I, "to inhabit an unknown country."
Jan Wyss, *The Swiss Family Robinson*

We too went   heads on pillows   bodies stretched out as if
adrift in canoes   new heavens opening through closed
eyelids   known leaves unfurling from dreamt branches   the
　　roots

of our most potent dream   a basswood's   anchored above
the derelict hillside orchard's scraggly survivors
its spire the lone bulwark left from the fruit trees' windbreak

broken by a century of northwesterlies   its
unexpected blossom-scent calling us up to it
on that first late June hill-walk   well before our ears caught

the hum of its shimmering crown of bees   or our eyes
blinked at sunset-glitter reflected a thousandfold
on wind-lifted undersides of heartshaped leaves   the tree

from then on stored in the mind's larder   and fetched into
pith by a distant knocking of woodpeckers homing
and foraging in its hollows   their ancestral keep

until toppled by a storm one August   in return
for the windfall of basswood our carpenter-neighbour
carved us a bedstead   frame of a little house   siderails

sturdy as rafters spanning our bedroom's plank floor from
spool-turned footboard to routed headboard   whose
    intricate
ripples and swirls set the whole construct afloat   fluted

Haida prow   our hands trawled the calm waters of its grain
a silt-bedded stream's hazy beige silk tester   and when
we slept on it the currents of our breath carried us

back to the tree   made whole again   back and into it
as if through the doorway and up the winding staircase
the Swiss family carved in their giant tree   earthbound

yet climbing to the source of honeyed dreams   and when we
made love in the creaking bedstead   our homecoming was
peck and *peck* and then sweet takeoff into the heavens

FOUR BRICK HOUSES

For Maurizio Trotta, architect and builder

Bricks are heavenly   Maurizio's fellow builder
Matisse Enzer ventures   a teasing gambit   more wise-
crack than staked claim   you think   for what could be
    more earthy

than brick   but he's in earnest   in full flight over the
infinite glimmerings of their sandy flanks   ripples
aquiver yet flameproof as angel wings   and as your

gaze coasts along Maurizio's moulded bricks you too
think *sky*   russet blush you've caught in July sunrises
confirming the upward thrust of his four houses   each

a thin hand raised in the peace gesture   far as can be
from Frank Lloyd Wright's American frontier reach   those
    ground-
hugging ranches expanding horizonward over

endless prairie   unfit for infill in a crowded
immigrant city   this plan a pure Canadian
compromise   neither eagle's span nor European

sparrows' cramped rows   graveled walkways running
    between walls
tree-canopied courtyards at back   and streetside no lawns
but tapestries of ivy hugging facades where bays

embrace the light with tall casements which   when opened
  send
shimmers of reflected brick upwards   wing-petals of
angels ascending to the pitched roof's attic dreamspace

HOLDINGS

Miniature bronze ballerina   a gift to her
mother from Giacometti himself   pair of Swiss bells
Deirdre cuddled to smuggle home from boarding school   each

    with little brass owls-head handle   sea-turtle snuffbox
    (ivory lid balanced on gold flippers   lift the hinged
    shell for the franked stamps kept inside)   set of twelve
      Meissen

        demitasse presented when Giselle first danced
          Giselle
        to great acclaim in Vienna   although *très intime*
        Deirdre's studio apartment holds the cherishings

of two lifetimes   hers and her mother's   intermingling
in the avian egg collection   grouped around real
blown specimens shipped from the exotic capitals

    Giselle toured   and greatly enlarged by Deirdre's
      carved wood
    enameled replicas   doubles but for the thin shells'
    lightness when lifted   Deirdre loves their wholeness
      the per-

fect sphere of an owl's egg you can cradle in your
    hand
loves their instinctive artistry   the linked strokes
    and whorls
on a red-winged blackbird's egg   so reminiscent of

cave paintings' leaping figures   her absolute favourite
the Brazilian guira   where an extra protective
layer forms a lacy white shawl draping the blue egg

the guira unlike other cuckoos no predator
but a nest-builder   its species name *guira guira*
easy to remember   sounding like *toora loora*

the lullaby her Irish nanny Bridget would sing
Deirdre to sleep with   the child snuggled in the
    folds of
a fluffy costume that gave off the mother's perfume

OPENWORK

While the face faded into the black screen   its last words
lingered   but *touch* was what she couldn't *keep in*   though
     not
for want of trying   those Skype sessions starting out as

porticos she might talk her way through   but morphing to
closed windows offering only her own retreating
smile   no more a cure for homesickness than the enlarged

photo   framed sample of dawn from their back porch   the
     known
place grown utterly foreign in this solitary
confinement   the mock-orange bush missing scent   its
     leaves un-

flappable   unswooped-on by the barn swallows who would
     weave
mud   mouthful by mouthful   into eave nests every spring
a scene uncurtained by cross-stitched snowflakes or the
     sheers

a wolf-spider would hang between spindles of porch-rail
yet now   open sesame   crocheted real curtains turned
the highrise's cold plate glass into home   Irish lace

her mother had slipped into her suitcase   the pair lay
dormant all summer under scarves and gloves   too narrow
to span the window   held up to it now they warmed her

deeper than wool   not because they could carry her back
to her old room   or the older room where her mother's
grandmother's hands threaded a hook through stenciled
    daisies

but because their openwork embraced the shapes outside
in little hugs of picot and chain   the neighboring
building knowable brick by brick   each of its sparrows

perched on a miniature ropebridge   some grown crow-sized
through raindrops   the cotton web a framework of soft
    bone
for the window's life to wind around and touch her own.

TRANSPLANT

Sometimes you need to pick a place up and replant it
if it is to grow   start with the flagstone sidewalk slabs
prise them out   heft them like stacked books with engraved
   titles

worn away   do not worry that such tomes will be too
ponderous   for memory is a thickly muscled
weightlifter   turn next to the stucco wall   its bottle-

green flank as unflowering as an iceberg's   its arched
black doorway frowning under a cowl of wedge-cut blocks
let the water of your eye float them free   and after

rolling up the starless sky above them like a bolt
of tarpaper   peel off the red patch from the second-
storey window   that hearth hanging fire on the air

and carry it in your breast pocket to a new land
where you will lower it into the hole pain has drilled
into your heart's subsoil   there the blood-rich seed will root

and send up fruited vines strong enough to frame afresh
the stones   the house   the sky   and the doorway you will
   now
enter to climb lit stairs and warm your hands at the hearth

REPURPOSING

The phoebe's eye   a star-kindled coal   lights on the base
of a rusted hurricane lantern and sees that un-
chimneyed hearth housing the nest she will weave like
    smoke from

moss and weed stems   while the carolina wren's crevice-
sweeping gaze recasts the crook of a tin pot canti-
levered from an icicle-draped window frame   into

her nestlings' cradle   and the ruby-throated humming-
bird   undaunted as white noise blizzards from power lines
over her wing-throbs   transmutes the frozen sea-green spume

of a glass insulator   with her tiny lens's
laser   into a soft hollow where small-bodied heat
can warm two snowdrop eggs to life   who says metaphor

is solely a lettered human art   if metaphor
means seeing within something that is   something that is
not yet   birds thread it through air with every flight   pleating

grass into high-pitched roundels   turning horsehairs into
the enjambed lines of their collections   the cliff swallow
a model of Virgilian patience   transposing

mouthful by mouthful   clay to build its monuments   swifts
like mystical poets   spinning steep nests from their own
insides   these compositions infused with touchable

substance such as earthbound singers can only aspire
to shape from the airy wisps of words   what wonder then
that others of our species   gatherers like the birds

can like them repurpose the world's denser offerings
and warm the smallest spaces with the eye's power to
transform   as Daniel in his one-room sixth-floor walkup

refires old bricks by filling each round hollow with wax
and wick   or peels labels to release gleam from empty
soup tins that send blue brimmings of lobelia over-

flowing onto an end table whose top once windowed
a lean-to and whose bicycle-wheel legs splay after-
noon sun into webbed glitter-nests on his wall   while Jen

two flights down   sets lamplight streaming through the
    wooden slats
of an inverted wastebasket onto the bookcase
she has framed from a stepladder   her books extending

the ladder's reach beyond her low-ceilinged room
    the shelves
stretching its walls around clearings of space and mind   each
castoff reclaimed by these inner-city foragers

a chimney swift's egg that contains   written in darkness
beneath a shell of snow   the flickering early stars
its inmate   breaking through   will gather under spread wings

II

ROOMMATES

I traverse Minesing Swamp while clad in
carpet slippers, fathom Orr Lake without
toe-testing, track the long hill to Anten
Mills from Flos in well under a minute.

With my index finger I dam rivers,
block sideroads, raze local airports, a God-
zilla on the rampage who can cover
green conservation areas in red

with a swish of marker, even collapse
the whole township by folding up the map:
pathetic fall, hollow apocalypse –
my hold only a paper tiger's grip.

Maps endow us with the ghost of power,
putting phantom landscapes within our reach
where no winds gather, no tree towers or
spreads shade, and rivers never overleap

their fine blue lines. This township of the mind
defaces place, burying Snow Valley's
white crystals under black letters, drying
Marl Lake to parchment. Allenwood's been de-

foliated, and Rainbow Valley Road
flattened, losing both arc and dip. I need
to touch the scabrous bark of a white oak
whose roots are in the earth, not in D3

or H6, finger silk hairs from a burst
milkweed pod on the monarch-kindling shore
of Nottawasaga's warm bay. I thirst
for a long draught of unmapped Springwater.

FRAMING THE COSMOS

All around us in the night sky   circles and ovals
trace spiral flower petals on a blackboard with no
flat surface   no back wall   they orbit in a garden

so remote we must have fallen from it long ago
the buds of light we see   withering aeons before
we give them names   or try to map with grids their inter-

lacing dances   or to contain in our story lines
the wanderings of their fiery tongues   even the stars
drawn by our children are planes and edges   for we live

in a squared world   horizon a blade at right angles
to our vertical stance   house posts in a three-hundred-
sixty-degree cosmos sunk firmly at ninety   *true*

being *upright*   though our rooted earthly gardens sur-
round us with windings   the earth itself a spinning wheel
nature shaking off straight lines   its pitches all curves or

screwball change-ups   we thrive on rectitude   no dustballs
clinging to plumb-lined walls   no puddled rainfall tempting
the up-and-up of an A-frame's halved orthogonal

we and our handiwork standing alone except for
the one straight shooter   light   without whose level columns
the canopy of stars would sink in darkness   without

whose transfusions of direct current there would be no
gardens   and no us   for all the square meals on our flat-
planed tabletops are take-out from the sun's lunch counter

the plants and plant eaters that we eat mere couriers
of light preserved from an unswerving stream   at its banks
all flesh drinks energy and makes matter   theirs and ours

shafts of stored sun balanced on earth's ball   but we alone
granted beams of reflection sturdy enough to frame
a door with parallel lights   giving onto the source

WHO FIRST

"The Greeks were eating pizza when the Italians were
living in caves"   so Eleftheria parried to
save face in face of her daughter's passion for Little

Italy's red-domed rendition of pita   her claim
tenuous as the strings of mandolins dismissed as
bouzouki knockoffs   because back when both clans cowered

under limestone domes   no one baked bread   and tomatoes
hadn't quit South America's shores   nobody knows
who first rolled dough   who took the first steps out of
    the cave

though we all first lived in the same house and still live there
dome-roofed shell   with small arched doorways open on
    both sides
to wind and song   a shared accommodation   nest for

the *who* of night-owl and the *who* of mourning dove   joint
tenants in a house not of timber but of timbre
and purveyors of food to a soul housed who knows where

TRANSMIGRATIONS

Imperious Caesar, dead and turned to clay,
Might stop a hole to keep the wind away.

Hamlet, 5.1

Or might be mouthed by a house martin   to be spit out
as a teardrop-shaped daub for the wall of its mud hut

just as a drop of Caesar's blood might be sucked into
the stabbing hypodermic shaft of a mosquito

to be in turn pecked and swallowed by a chickadee
and become   from plunging through its alimentary

ductwork   part of the shell housing an embryonic
black-capped chick   which will use its pointed egg-tooth
    to pick

a hole in the wall   recycling the shell's calcium
into a wingbone riding winds to its winter home

but you   Hamlet   homeless wanderer in the boneyard
pick up a hollow gourd   wind-harrowed cave   abandoned

nest of your childhood   clay too brittle to be reworked
and wish the jester could be repurposed   unburdened

of memory   that he might house only next spring's fresh
songs   echo-free   no sparrows fallen on the threshold

PROSERPINA

Like a little old lady whose years have compressed her
into a dwarf of the debutante whose feathered gown
peacocked across the dance floor   this turkey vulture sits

hunched   shoulders withdrawn into folds of a way-too-big
black cloak   sparse frizz exposing a sunburned scalp
    furrowed
like the forehead below it   wouldn't you be worried

too if you were married to Death   nested in under-
growth   fed with life's leftovers   starved of song   utterly
surprising then to look up and see the bird cartwheel

on wings as wide and elegantly long-feathered as
those Angelico painted on angels   see her tip-
sily hang-gliding or riding sunwards   *no hands*   up

the thermals' invisible fire-poles   propelled by
pure joy   for like Angelico's Gabriel she too
brings happy news of a greening   hers also rising

from a plundered garden   winter having deflowered
all the bright-plumed maidens   but for her the
    underworld's
harrowing calls up miraculous birth   earth's return

no special delivery from a star   but promised
in the bouquet her husband sends her   and scenting there
in mid-career the fragrance of next spring   she plunges

where he too drinks   swooping into the drive-thru as swifts
dip down to skim pools   his rimmed with paper   its surface
rippled with brown bubbles   and where he too eats   beakless

but open-mouthed   popping down not gnats but sugared
    scraps
his nest no swift's cup woven of floating dried grass drawn
from the air   but a frayed vinyl captain's chair cushioned

with taped-on towels   where he sits only on the rounds
of himself   what keeps him from landing isn't a swift's
weak vestigial feet   but want of a perch near the un-

flowering plant that claims his days   so he migrates through
long miles of morning and evening darkness   chorused with
chatter or static   far from the swifts' airborne matings

as from the back-seat couplings of youth   his worst
    nightmare
dozing off in mid-flight   his dream   their sleep on the wing
their feathers caressed by winds that keep them from falling

GROUNDED

from the German of Durs Grünbein

Never liftoff, these pecs
weak as emu or ostrich.
Ribs too hefty, gormless
limbs not springy enough.
Standing at the window, elbows
akimbo, tracing a gull's
plunge, hurts like a toothache.
Arcs, ovoids, ampersands
floor you, number one on
the endangered list, Long-
Necked Invalid. Only
a penguin can stand it, wings
twitching, dreams lofty.

CREATURE LONGINGS

We can buy nests woven from bungees and bean canes   from
eucalyptus branches tough as tungsten when cured   or
choose a softer option from supple maple saplings

or   for the eco-conscious   looped skeins of old tires
leather scraps   smudged poly shipping-container strapping
whatever weave knits us back into the primal web

our overcomplicated heartstrings quiver for   cowled
outpost   giving onto open grassland planted in
our eyes   when they peered from under ape-brows
    unburdened

with baggage   those roosts like songbird nests no sooner
    used
than yielded   yet the nook we really hanker after
lies beneath the furred or feathered brow   the creature's

brain-housing   domed haunt of senses beyond
    the threshold
of our own   land of Oz where the smallest chickadee's
lens widens with otherworldly rainbows   where inner

ears of fieldmice surf on waves of infinite thinness
and bees become their own divining rods homing on
nectar by riding magnetic currents   what dancer's

entrechat can rival the shimmer of a goldfinch
lighting upwards on a twig as if every grounding
were a further flight   the bird's mind a winged undoing

of gravity   brain as impenetrable to our
flat-footed thinking as the nest it winds from thistle
and milkweed   catkin and grass   so tightly it can sail

shipshape through summer storms   while hatchlings
    feather themselves
into little weavings   loops of the yellow skein that
can burn our skin and turn it cancerous as envy

SERPENTS ON A WALNUT CROSIER

They live within us   a tenancy first suggested
by this wood   whose fruit's whorled and fissured centre traces
in small the rounded clefts of the brain's canyoned terrain

where thought-snakes coil and dart   slipping into shadowy
chinks to rise   like waterspouts sheathed in gleam   from deeper
crevasses of their bifurcated home whose twoness

matches both our doubled eyes   ears   hands   and the twin loops
of this serpent pair who   lacking the limbed instruments
for capture   concentrate it into the fanged and mouthed

tubes of their bodies   all reach-and-eat   and most human
in their legendary greed for immortality
shucking off worn lives like creased pyjamas in endless

reawakenings   hissing at mortal limits with
the s's of their bodies   even a holy man
trudging along   legs grateful for a staff   might envy

them their easy resurrections   were his eyes not trained
like theirs on the cross between them   and on the figure
invisible but understood as nailed to it   stretched

in two directions   legs pointing downward to an in-
escapable earth   arms spreading outward in an all-
embracing love his human flesh consents to die for.

EMBRACE

The embrace of prayer does not annihilate
like Jupiter's embrace of Semele
whose pleas for god met with incineration,
or that of Raven who, hungering to be
enlightened, swallowed the sun and plunged Creation
into darkness deeper than feathered ebony.

Think instead how earth and sun enfold
each other, each one holding its own spin,
yet, like two dancers, both together held
in heavenly rhythm – earth lending body to sun's
light turns, sun twirling over earth's shoulder
a fiery scarf in perfectly timed rounds.

Or think of the embrace in which you share
when reading, the feathery lines awakened, moved
to spin in your eyes' light, your thoughts a sphere
encompassing the whirling flight paths of
no swooping raven but a broad-winged dove,
a prayer who has become one with the prayer.

THE GATE

Nature's immortals do not share your fixation
with limits. Air comes and goes slick as a whistle
through midnight drapes as through the sheers of noon,
slipping down into your lungs for a warm kiss

or surfing the cool wind-waves above walls.
Water rolls over shorelines, melting into sand
and rock alike. Fire's hundred-fingered hands
thread the carved spume of spindles, yet can bull-

doze buildings into its roaring mouth. Even
earthbound trees reach into unfenced clearings
of sky, mortal leaves chatting, oblivious,
ablush as autumn leads to white closure –

and what doomed sparrow does not trust its wings
will always lift it over the tallest hedge?
Only your eyes survey the acreage
of infinity and find a shut gate waiting.

Chainlinked with death, you garden the enclosed
expanse, tend air and name it with your breath,
make rain your sorrow's whispers to an earth
that cannot give voice to its own deep thirst,

and train the flames of your rage to speak as roses.
Minding leaf cadences that escape a tree's
cupped lobes, you call them song. Reading the thrust
of rising beak and wing in swooping leaves,

you call up coming spring through autumn's cage
where, from a fallen tree, you carve a gate,
place a hand on it, turn it like a page,
and enter a garden waiting for you beyond it.

It's perched within hailing distance   but your loudest shout
won't reach this earless figure   and merely to say *treed*
distorts a nature thought to be unnatural   roots

a floating mystery   so instead you start with pure
abstraction   and your eye makes out that most platonic
pairing of perfect round with perfect straight   a cone   yet

closer looking fractures this notion   reveals a rift
jagged as an earthquake splitting the cone from apex
to base   earthy too the ripples running from the fault

transversely down the cone   like those inscribed on a beach
after the tide withdraws   as if the figure lifted
the top layer of sand and wrapped it around itself

for a robe   whose folds are breached now   the fabric parting
as   from the abandoned darkness   appear a newly
emergent swallowtail's wet wings   joined over a heart

whose beachhead is the whole body   and whose tides will un-
furl striped silk water-lights   fluttering like leaves   to fan
the nectar from rooted flowers up to the heavens

WHITE OVER BLUE

Wing it, butterfly,

rippling concentration of

the soul of the lake.

OLD SOUL

Olygyra oribiculata   your name's dance on
our tongue's floor starts out soft shoe   labial and liquid
but ends tapping flamenco heel percussives   is this

your history   pea-sized snail   once a thin-skinned shuffler
swaying on the early Cambrian tide   whose salt sting
bruised you into such deep seclusion   you felt no house

secure except one spun from your own core   flesh toughened
to ironstone   arteries to veins of ore   yet not
without a dancer's grace   as you balance a castle

on your back   its turret a whorled dome whose spiral course
follows the unrolling of our galaxy   is this
partnering why you're content to move at a snail's pace

or to withdraw from all motion behind a sealed door
not because you fear the stars' fury   but because you
enfold that old flame beneath the faint blush of your shell.

Granite bulwarked, spruce turreted, it would be their own moated castle, walled by deep water from the treacherous shallows of postwar America. Or a pirate-free Treasure Island. Perhaps even – with swaying crow's nests – a broad-hulled million-masted *Hispaniola* they alone would command, both vessel and port. Or a blank-leafed book waiting to be storied in the rainbow ink of unconstrained imagination.

Yet the pages set aside for triumphant arrival had thinned out by their first autumn, grown deciduous and brittle as falling red-maple leaves, incarnate with departure. The deed of ownership – once proud supernova atop their mainland Christmas tree – morphed into a white paper moon, dim in an island orbit where possession was questioned by sea winds storming through wood-shingled walls, or by the rise and heavy fall of tidal rage on stone beach shingles.

Even the sea's gifts proved elusive, more often heard than seen, as when the dory – unmoored in a squall, captive to fog filling up vistas their saw-blades had opened – drummed its position in response to waves that knocked its sides, calling out bulk and bearings, sounding a leaden void.

The land itself was haunted by presences harder to ignore than the earlier human settlers whose names wind and rain had taken, their grave-slabs wiped as free from tenancy as the foundation stones Art and Nan quarried for garden paths. Now more insistent claimants left calling cards on the air. Reek of fresh scat from vanished deer. Ripple of dust-motes, construed over time as wake of a meadow vole sailed out of sight in high grass. Whisked-back green shimmer of tongue behind granite teeth (aura of garter-snake).

Most unsettling: the calls of birds, unseen among forest roof-beams, but persistent. Incorrigible other, not to be coaxed into the human fold no matter how many veils of the famil-iar gathered around their cries. The yellow-throated warbler vaulted beyond the squeaking wheel it called to mind. The junco's alarm was breath-rooted, blooded, like no bedside clock. Thrush song resisted translation into *pure sweet sweet beauty* of language.

How surprising then, in their second year – though too slow an unfolding for them to *feel* surprised – when duets arose between the birds' rhythms and theirs, set to bird-measure. Hammer on nail became a duffer's blunt accompaniment to the woodpecker's deft strokes. Bucksaw rasped against the grain straining to keep pace with the tufted titmouse's airy cross-cuts. The ups and downs of their tobogganing played in the inner ear to the tune of a black-capped chickadee climbing and sliding down its hills of air.

A mysterious near-bridging of distances, ever elusive,
brought closest contact not with those feathered breathfuls
of life, but with more broad-ribbed, antlered islanders –
whitetail deer whose songs of silence or fading hoofbeats
took decades to learn: caught in steam rising from body-
warmed earthen circles, or heard when crouched out of
sight beneath a windowsill, inches from paw-thrusts in moon-
lit snow and frenzied bouts of gulping down the found grass.
And when, with bread or apples set where clearing met
spruce forest, they fed that hunger, they were nourished.

The communion of separateness, touching beyond touch,
grew more intimate after his death. A whitetail guided her
home from her forest of grief, as in an old-fashioned dance
– no bodily contact, but leading and following, breathing the
air each other's breath warmed. And later, from a window in
the mainland nursing home, before her ashes mingled with
his on the island, wasn't her eyes' embrace with those of a
buck on the fenced lawn their true reunion?

PAPER COVERS ROCK*

Stone becomes rounded   by the action of weather and
waves   it takes information from water   but very
slowly   paper is quicker   so over the sea-rocks

she drapes scarves of paper   gauze dressings for abrasions
splits and deep fissures   wounds in the clenched brawn of
   these sleek-
skinned sentries   from the long siege of wind and tide that
   still

pound the battlements   paper consoles rock with silky
massages and the unfolding story of its soon
dwindling life   this quick study shivered to shreds by wave

upon wave   and because she knows the fragility
of paper's passages   her own life a mere shutter-
flick compared to the rock's delayed exposure   she sets

down the stories of both on fresh paper   first with light
and later with flecks of ink that   when encountered by
the Beothuk   must have looked like black-spotted clutches

of salmon eggs   themselves so frail   some clawed by crayfish
from river gravel   some trampled into it by hoof
or paw   but like fry whose rifeness ensures survival

this letter-spawn thrives through profusion   myriad kin
outlasting waves of breath   resisting the suck of tide
toward dissolution   covering stone with awareness

of stone's deep past   telling family histories of
rocks parted by continental drift   envisioning
rock's future when time has scissored all paper away

The clan has gathered here for millions of years   millions
upon millions of us kinfolk   all descended from
the shotgun marriage of hydrogen and helium

all of us   whether curly-haired or hairless   green-eyed
or eyeless   knowable from the rhythm at our core
the round dance pairing adenine with thymine   guanine

with cytosine   passed down through the whole family like
cleft chins or widow's peaks   each of us embracing the
other for dear life   rooted and unrooted donning

one another's hand-me-down breath   all nursed by barter
nectar traded in exchange for strewing of pollen
clownfish granting protection from butterfly fish   to

anemone giving clownfish protection from shark
all of us living off light   some rays taken in whole
and turned to sweetness by leaf-mouth   some spread like
    warm cloaks

and winked back moonlike from wet skin or scale   some
    kindled
by photocytes sparking deep-sea dragonfish lanterns
or tiny airborne torches of fireflies   but your light

burns unique   for only the humans in this mansion
carry   in the bone lantern of the head   the glimmer
of suns yet to rise or set   only yours the gift of

wider consciousness   only you can keep watch over
all the kinfolk   not their grand sire but *avunculus*
the "little grandfather"   the protector   the uncle.

SONNETS TO ORPHEUS, 2:1

from the German of Rainer Maria Rilke

Breathing, you poem lost to sight!
Constant turnover
of Being with pure world-room. Counterweight
through whose rhythms I occur.

Unbroken wave whose
sea I slowly become;
most thrifty of all possible seas –
on ground reclaimed.

How many of these places in space were once
inside me. Many a wind
is like my son.

Can you recognize me, air, home to my kinfolk?
You, once sleek bark,
rondure and leaf of what I spoke.

SHARED ACCOMMODATIONS

No one ever lives alone   the most remote apart-
ment is at its core a withment   even if you're off
the grid   neither aglow with copper currents borne from

distant cascades   nor tapping the reservoir's coiled roots
of pipework   the breeze that spins your windmill and gives
    lift
to your lungs' wings high-fives you with skyward-reaching
    breath

from all your animal cousins and their green forbears
while the stream you drink sweet-talks your lips with kisses
    from
mist-brewing mountains   and the little house in your chest

owes its ruby walls to the same hematite that streaks
earth's deepest caves with rust   even in the labyrinth
of your dreaming brain   you are no more alone than a

single starling in a flock navigating sudden
cloudshifts after sunset   or one small fry in a school
of herring silvering blue depths   each swerve of impulse

reverberating through air or water or chambers
of the mind   those mirror-hung corridors whose faces
are yours and every other body's   all your roommates

III

FLYWAYS

POLAR VISIONS*

1. Forty Umbrellas, 1818

Picture this   two black birds larger than whales come gliding
across the snow-maned waves   fold many pairs of upright
white wings   then float at rest   you and the other hunters

given this apparition   wonder if the creatures
have flown from the sun or from the moon   for nothing on
earth grows so high over it   and when men in blue pelts

who ride their backs   paddle ashore in boats to tell you
the birds are wooden houses   you do not believe them
since wood is a scattered tribe of reeds and slats   neither

strong for walls like winter ice   nor plentiful for tents
like caribou   you accept their gifts of dark water
to drink   and powder to breathe up the nose   and only

when you unfold their useless small black tents do you see
something you know   ribs carved from baleen of the
    bowhead
the whale that gives you food and warmth and light   and
    that will

become as scarce as European forests   plundered
to timber sailing ships whose wood housed   in its ringed ribs
the life of a thousand suns   from long days of summer

2. *Croker's Mountains, 1818 & 1833*

Now picture this   a wall of mountains blocking the sought
northwest passage   baptize them for the Admiralty's
First Lord   ink them on your charts   head the *Isabella*

homewards   you are John Ross   bestower of brandy   snuff
and forty umbrellas   to the "Arctic Highlanders"
you faced on crags of sea-ice   your face next year stony

but red when your lieutenant   making air of granite
sails through mountains   that you *distinctly saw* in weather
too clear for fog and cloud to stack the horizon with

mirage   those cliffs no trick of sight   but solid refuge
from what your diary tries to contain in wobbly
palisades of black ink   *monotonous waste   silence*

and death   where nothing moves and nothing changes   now fast
forward fifteen years   past the icebound and abandoned
Victory of your second expedition   to where

you and your crew   given up for dead   tattered sealskins
over rag-ends of dress blue   *starved to the very bones*
turn oars to wings and catch the sole sail glimpsed in four
    years

whaler   square-rigged   once naval   the same *Isabella*
you had commanded   the mountain of black wood waiting
a migratory creature returned to home waters

3. Antarctic Centaur, 1911

No need to picture this   you've done it for us   snapping
a photo before sledging from Ross Island across
the ice towards the pole and your death   leader of the doomed

Scott Expedition   none of your crew caught here with
these wide-eyed blanketed ponies   the three in profile
more like men in horse costume   two sets of leather boots

propping each blanket   but the fourth   *en face*   distinctly
mythical   its stem of booted legs rising into
the cloth-circled waist   then flowering as a horse's

neck and head   a South Pole centaur   appropriately
inverted   human below and equine above   what
could this creature be thinking   do its eyes   larger than

those of man or whale   take in the prairie grass for whose
sweet scent its flared nostrils search   do they foresee the death
of all your ponies   some drowned   some shot then skinned
    and made

into tents   or do they brim with reproach for eyes that
lacking horse-sense   have gone wandering through ranges
    of
lost victory   grassless   icebound   distant as the moon

AT THE CORNER OF OIL AND BEEF

Sturgis Motorcycle Rally, Sturgis, South Dakota

More than magenta tattoos   that flicker action films
of flame-snorting dragons or sea serpents across once
muscled chests   shoulders   forearms   more than massive
  rhinestone

encrusted buckles   studding barrel-waisted denims
with ersatz Mayan bling   their headgear blazes longings
to return to a more fabled age   Viking helmets

some horned   some winged with stripes or lightning
  bolts   golden clasped
bandanas   starred midnight or blood red silks that
  might have
fringed the brow of Blackbeard or Long John Silver   and
  most

of all   the towering broad-brimmed stetsons   mesas on
the move   their shadows sweeping once-vast plains under
  wheeled
riders' great horsepowered mounts   mythology of man

versus steer   as potent as the frescoed bull-leapers
on Cretan walls   and here on Sturgis Main Street   near One-
Eyed Jack's Saloon   where curbed Electra Glides and
  Road Kings

idle under *Texas Beef Brisket   Deep Fried Sirloin*
Tips   and *ribs ribs ribs*   mingling fumes   where no one
   reckons
the sixteen pounds of grain gone up in smoke for each pound

of meat   or the ninety tons of antique plant matter
hecatombed in every gallon of gas   I long to
satisfy these cowboys' longings a million times o-

ver   send them back way beyond Minoan rodeos
beyond the first taming of cattle   the first sowing
of grain that fed them   beyond the first rooted earthlife

to pirate-free ancient seas beneath the plains   before
titanic heat gods spirited oil   from the micro-
scopic remains of floating protoplankton   before

each diatom and dinoflagellate burned sunshine
to carbon   send these steersmen back   hands whisked
   from throttle-
grips   haunches from hand-tooled leather saddles   back
   beyond

the blinding glitter of their gas-fed longhorns' chrome flanks
in mythic ascension   to untracked starry passes
where light glides   flameless   smokeless   tinged only with
   promise

TWEET

High on the cathedral … amid a phalanx of stone statues …
one of the angels … is chatting on a cellphone.

New York Times, 5 March 2012

In the beginning were birds   from green-fringed watchtowers
catching the yet unrisen sun's first signal   drawing
it out as song   invisible stream that entered night-

chilled ears and filled us with rose-warmth   or after sunset
tending a glow of feathers against the sky's black ice
guardians of colour   cradled candles flickering

red and gold   or in midday flocking up from shade-tiled
woodland floor to graze the open blue   then when we
    brought
down the forest   missing its wing-thronged pillars   we cast

as their stand-ins marble columns   that ramified where
squared slabs met in place of the canopy's woven roof
and grey-fledged angels kept a soundless vigil   over

the stained glass windows' brittle plumage   fringed with
    carved leaves
forever stilled in frost   each buttressed grove no trellis
for nests but the ribbed rampart of an entrenchment   dawn

chorus dwindling to a single species-call   further
narrowed now into a lightless cell   cold as the hand
that cradles it against an ear stone deaf to birdsong

SACRED SPACE

Not till we are lost … do we begin to find ourselves, and
realize where we are and the infinite extent of our relation.
                                        Thoreau, *Walden* (VIII:2)

All lost   the trees whose stirred leaves' whispers choired
    as one
with the enchanting plainsong of goddesses whose hair
was windcombed branches   the groves where tree crowns
    canopied

floors on which dancing foot and leaf-shadow threaded
    through
each other's quickened turns   the forests of trees and groves
lost to the bite of ancient axes hewing out masts

for fleets now planted on seabeds   or lost to raindrops
laden with newer stem-and-leaf-eating ruin   lost
also the temples whose columns rose in place of trees

and dancing reed-crowned nymphs   all rubble   one trunk
    remains
of Artemis's sacred shrine leveled with other
haunts of eternity   buckled into time like you

borne down by your lost haven   feeling yourself a lone
fallen caryatid shouldering mortality   yet
you are not your marble burden   deep rooted in time

you live more wood-nymph than stone   the very air you
    breathe
rounding on itself in choral dance   lungs embracing
breath that quickens life upon life from mouth to stoma

to nostrils   tidal rhythm where each fresh wave renews
an earth-enfolding ocean   timeless within time's rounds
whether the breath unsinkable surges without sound

or the mouth shapes it into singing words   like leaf veins
that print a tree's windturned pages with life-giving lines
like sky-bearing streams over which all space is sacred.

THE GUIDE SPEAKS*

"Wouldn't it sink   an ark timbered with stone pillars   railed
with arches of square-cut masonry?"   answer's no   though
not for reasons our age might give   we'd say it's merely

a stained glass window panel   not Noah's real vessel
the artist if he chose could have depicted an ark
of crystal   still no risk of shipwreck   no tidal surge

lapping through those squiggly strokes beneath   but we'd
    be wrong
about the kind of ark the medieval artist's mind
sailed in   here's a hint   you're sitting in it now   this nave

the word means ship   floats on voyages of the spirit
in a fourth dimension beyond the three we touch   if
pillars and arches sink into the earth   this ship still

will be seaworthy because it sails with us   both here
and elsewhere   let me ask you   pardon my pointing   you
young man in blue blazer   third row   where do you live
    have

you stopped living since you're no longer in Boston   or
have you brought it with you   don't you carry it around
inside you   just as this cathedral roams through me   how

else could I talk about the windows behind my back
while looking at you   so now that we've solved the weighty
problem of the ark   let's return to my earlier

question   why a green cross in the redemption window
yes   good for you   you're becoming more at home in that
fourth dimension   Christ's passion greens the wood of
    the cross

no matter what season   it offers the believer
spring   we could stop at this point in the tour   having left
space and time behind us   but let's make one more leap
    look

up to the second lancet window   at King David
strumming a harp   we can't hear the music   not because
it's just a picture but because his ten strings   count them

sing beyond the human octave's range until the Last
Judgement purifies our ears   those finer notes for now
float unheard   like the ark   but like the ark they move us

through light   the windows all together playing a kind
of silent symphony   David's gold crown radiant
in response to Christ's   Mary's blue veil in harmony

with the heavens   isn't that what the John the Divine
panels are all about   those pieces of glass sounding
a music for the eye   as in his Gospel when Word

changes to Light   which is as good a place as any
to leave off   thank you for your patience   you're very kind
but no   I fear my words are mostly just breath   fated

with candle smoke to darken walls and windows   I've grown
into the statue of that other John outside   bent
and weatherbeaten   yet   yes   content to bear witness

with words that will never hold the pure white answer   of
the dove's wings returning to the ark   my words more like
the script the wrens unwrite in writing it on the sky.

He might insist he's just Bill Cunningham   *New York Times*
glamour tracker   fashion-photo snapper   portraitist
of peacock plumage   might remind you that he   though
    raised

Catholic   has like the Church itself no truck with re-
incarnation   but don't believe him   believe instead
in him   take the duct-tape-patched poncho for the saint's
    thread-

bare tunic   corded with a Nikon's case strap   the bike
stalled upright in the closet for his tethered donkey
see his tiny flat niched in the echoing rockwalls

of midtown   as the blessed Francis's cell   dresser-
less in the absence of any concern for raiment
chairless in disdain of creature comfort   his pantry

elsewhere as those of the birds of the field who   like him
subsist on takeout   like them he lives to wing it with
the angels   hummingbird flick of his shutter shot through

with iridescence glanced off damask   chiffon   lamé
ascetic lens abstaining from focus on fabric
or beneath it   transfixed in unbodied communion

with split-second hosts of light untainted by the dark
ages pressed into earthly diamonds   these brilliants free
from time's burdens   as he from matter's weight   uplifted

on bicycle wheels that wink back sunbeams and headlights
through their chrome lenses   no more a capture   he knows
    than
happens in a Nikon's heart   and he no more a saint

than in his contentment with negatives   flimsy in-
versions   translucent mists filling the filing cases
that line his apartment   ask him about religion

and like his medieval double he's speechless   having
given up those words   those souvenirs littering the
avenues between him and the real   those negatives

THE HOUSE OF MYTH:
IN MEMORY OF NORTHROP FRYE

*Mythical animals ... may be as essential for society as mythology itself ...
as characteristic for human beings as nest-building is for birds. The stories
seem to be different stories, but the underlying structure is always the same,
in any part of the world, at any time.*

Lewis Thomas

One of its distinguishing properties is to be
without property   no visible means of support
comings and goings unencumbered as they have been

through all times and places   from mouthblown dioramas
of Paleolithic hollows to the wind-unfurled
pennants configured on inaccessible mountains

spied by satellite   yet some highly documented
urban encounters in modern central Canada
mention a portal surmounted by flared oriel

flanked by frameless windows   the house roofed in thatch
    described
as gold weathered to grey   accounts vary on whether
it stands or rocks gently on its footings   what is known

of the interior   scholars have pieced together
from shards of paper that seem to have drifted down from
regions far above the house's higher stories   all

confirm however a vestibule that leaves no room
for small talk   giving way abruptly in a cascade
of stone steps to the core of the building   likened by

as many sources to a vast furnace room as to
a hall of ice or a salt mine   these discrepancies
no doubt symptoms of the same disorientation

that has identified such spaces the world over
with legends of a permeable wall   how the hand
of one explorer resting against roughcast passed through

and when pulled back out was a furred paw   how another's
foot emerged ungulate and cloven   as if the wall
possessed the power to erode evolved distinctions

between animal and human   in the manner that
the subterranean flood cited in the fullest
of crypt narratives causes those who breast its current

to turn amphibian   web-limbed and furnished with gills
for breathing the air at the heart of water   before
surfacing once more in human form at the ground floor

landing of the winding stair that is such houses' most
contentious feature   windpipe-like spiral belying
the straight lines of written site studies and extending

within   so far beyond the height gauged by external
purview as to end in the clouds   confusion reigns in
all the known records of these storied upper levels

yet however implausibly all evidence points
to a garden at the top of the stairs   where either
women named for flowers or flowers named for women

dance in unbroken rings around a dreamer rooted
in that place   his hair rippling leaves   his breath keeping
   time
with their quick steps   following them through closed
   eyes   bemused

FRESCO MAGIC

1. Pompeii

Look how they made walls vanish   not by running
   through them
Harry-Potter-style   but by painting them with what lay
beyond   hillsides of nimble-limbed olive trees dandling

clustered fruit from silver fingers   wind-furrowed
   wheatfields
squirrels lacing the nearby oak groves   and if you threw
wide the batten-framed shutters your eyes would be treated

not trumped   with flourishes setting inner and outer
in harmony   grace notes of lacquered vines in duet
with sun-gilded grapes   shadows bridging from garden dials

to gnomons atop enameled globes   not a still life
among them   all in motion   whether counterpointing
the sun's steady pace or quickened by the caperings

of torchlight   the builders not weighed down with all you
   know
about the heavy rain of pumice that melted roofs
muffled transoms and blinded windows   for they looked on

stone walls as wells of shifting light   their view not monu-
mental but moment-centred   waving wands of trowel
and brush to summon up a flute breathlessly upraised

for your fingering   or jug-eared Silenus reeling
from a column   or Aurora herself in mid-step
winking at you to join in the dance   now you see it

2. *Villa Cicogna Mozzoni*

His brother the Count and heir can't stand the place   too
    far
from Wi-Fi   women   and song   so Jacopo tends it
tending mostly meaning standing after the rains   perched

high on a rung   patching cracked stucco or shoring up
tipsy roof-tiles   to keep the damp from feasting on aged
plaster and making a velouté of the frescoes

composed in the 1560s by two craftsmen from
Cremona   whose art was brush rather than awl   and who
brought back through pigment-magic the century-old glow

of the Duke of Milan's visit   but Jacopo's most
cherished frescoes aren't *Young Agostino Mozzoni
Saves Duke Galeazzo from the Ferocious Bear*   or

the untitled bedroom panels whose red paint takes on
the nap and fall of velvet   or the hallway's presti-
digitation   where the marble balustrade your hand

reaches for dissolves into a flat mirror-image
of its solid counterpart   but rather those vistas
that open view on view like Russian dolls   the stone-browed

portal framing a hall whose floor tiles gleam with sunlight
from some unglimpsed window   and whose foreshortened
    walls frame
another hall   where three thin-thinner-thinnest rays lay

gold stripes across a narrowing blue runner that ends
before the smallest hall targets your eye on a nub
of window at its heart   or the scene most at *his* heart

perhaps because most exposed   outdoors where the
    arcade's
painted sky peeks through a painted trellis supporting
espaliered branches   bunches of grapes   and climbing
    hands

and feet of two putti grinning down from opposite
sides of the ceiling   each boy either upright or up-
side-down   grapes dangling or levitating   depending

on whose chubby-fingered grip you focus   Jacopo's
weathered hands touching all the magic   his feet knowing
the ache of keeping such laddered airiness aloft

CLUB OF ROME

from the German of Durs Grünbein

Departed Carthages behind his back, before his eyes
Snow-white, the Alps' elephant graveyard,
Wasn't the Roman a survivor from whom
Time ran out eastwards?

Catacombs underfoot, in whose dripping passageways
Fanatics camped, baking damnation
With their daily bread, wasn't fear of barbarians
The last-act magic?

While balustrades and vases glistened more brightly from
    every
Crack in the marble, doorsills worn down
Like whorehouse mattresses, from forest floors shot up
Hostiles like toadstools.

Shadows from the colder side of the moon lengthened over
Overgrown gardens. Pigs fattened
On sarcophagi. Through the groundwater dappled
Blood from the toilets.

Only the admired old patricians plotted zestfully over
Foreclosed property, their big game
Volleying between laughter and tears, their credo:
"After us, shit hits."

A BRIEF TOUR OF MURANO

Found poem, text taken from Rosa Barovier Mentasti,
Murano: The Glass-Making Island, Ponzano, 2006

The Basilica dei Santi Maria e Donato, the square named
after it, and the surrounding buildings have always been
Murano's religious and political centre ... not far away from
what was the very first church here, San Salvatore, which no
longer exists.

It is unfortunate that the Palazzo Podestarile, built in the
14th century and then rebuilt after a fire in the 16th century,
was razed to the ground in 1815 ... The medieval baptistery
... had already met with a similar fate in 1719.

The apsidal conch has a polychrome and gold mosaic por-
traying Our Lady, made in the 13th century, while the gable
of the apse, also decorated with a mosaic, was destroyed in
Baroque times.

Along the canals ... were ... palazzos and villas built by the
aristocratic families of Venice for the summer months. Only
a few traces of those elegant homes still remain, most of
them having been demolished.

The fresco that used to decorate the façade has now com-
pletely disappeared however some traces of the terracotta,
stucco and fresco work ... are still visible in the interior.

Near San Donato stood Palazzo Vendramin and the lavish Palazzi Corner, with a garden between them but linked by an arcade, later all razed to the ground.

Also beyond the Canal Grande of Murano … were the convents and churches of San Martino (11th century), of San Giacomo di Galizia (pre-14th century), of San Maffio (or Matteo, 11th century), of San Mattia (13th century) and of San Giuseppe (18th century). Anyone wanting to visit these old buildings, once full of works of art, would be disappointed. They have almost all disappeared … while the church of Santa Chiara … now an empty and run-down shell, is barely standing.

While most of the elements of the interior decoration, the frescoes, the stucco work and the furnishings have been lost, the borough has retained its fascination, due to its constant vitality … It is … well worth visiting, loving, investigating and photographing.

DETROIT

No way it's Pompeii   no matter how hard the guides on
foot or online push the kinship   no way a furrowed
upsurge of smudge from the unstorying of Hudson's

Department Store can match the molten tantrum that burst
from the lips of Vesuvius   no way water's crawl
through the Packard Motors Plant's peeling drywall can keep

up with the Indy-speed whoosh that razed and buried then-
and-there in a flash   this papyrus roll Ulysses
Ricci carved into the limestone façade of the now-

decaying Free Press Building holds no precious secrets
like those of its carbonized prototypes   or the casks
of ash that baked to stone around lit victims caught in

the surge   the slave holding a roof tile over his head
in the Garden of the Fugitives   the doorkeeper
crouched under pillows in the House of Menander   no

freeze-frame gestures here   for downtown Detroit is home to
no body   so this room in what might be called the House
of the Dentist takes hold of us with the power of

absence   the examination chair's headrest propping
no one's occipital bones   the unsipped cup   the lamp
tilting into nothing   as into a crater's mouth

REINCARNATIONS

The Inn of the Sixth Happiness was in fact the Inn
of Eight Happinesses   its starving Chinese orphans
well-fed and parented Liverpudlians   its loaved

peaks stand-ins on loan from Wales   its balsa pagoda
pure Hollywood   which also devalued the foundling
called "Ninepence" to "Sixpence"   all this factual slippage

forgivable in light of the reincarnations
wrought by its celluloid   the dying Robert Donat
his walk a shuffle   his voice mere chirp   not downsized to

a grasshopper like ancient Tithonus   but lifted
into immortality as the ermine-collared
oak-backboned Mandarin whose final *We shall not see*

each other again gets indefinitely postponed
each time his half-smile is rescreened   a transformation
doubled in Ingrid Bergman's figure   which not only

like Athena washing a gold sheen over the storm-
beaten silver of Odysseus   reshapes the short
Cockney original into a statuesque Swede

her nickname softened from A-weh-deh ("virtuous one")
to Jen-ai ("the one who loves people") in keeping with
the plot's coupling her with a handsome half-caste colonel

who'll be her happily-ever-after   but also
spares Bergman real life's last eight years of cancer   closing
with knick-knack happiness as she sings the orphans home

A fugitive among the unmagicked   he at first
anchored his faith in stone   piton driven into cliff
to haul himself skyward   wedge-shaped bolt lifting word-block

into the sentence's pointed arch   but what took place
up against walls and inside them   red seepage   red stains
the complicit silence of stone   drove him out into

the air   the poem no longer monument   now poised
on voice alone like vapour   a cast of lace   a catch
of breath in each stitched round   the poet's lips shaping
    words

unpenned   no notebooks needed   the printless works
    archived
only in memory's open stacks   until exile
sacked the city of his mind   shelf upon ghostly shelf

rifled and overturned   the words' swift flight from silence
to speech hijacked or aborted   he saw they needed
ink's river to reach safe harbour   black water drawn from

ground stone   burnt bones   sodden bark   words ferried
    by hand
on black-hulled arks like Egyptian funerary boats
fitted out for the long journey to their afterlife

RENEWALS

from the German of Durs Grünbein

As long as grass pushes up through the cracks
   Nothing is lost. The tree
Measures generations with thin rings.
   The burnt-out tenement
Leaves behind only a charred pit
   Or a fresh playground. Lightly
A kite climbs urban zephyrs of exhaust,
   Along the ashen puddles
Bobs a paper boat. How your heart soars
   When a squawking blackbird
Defends her bit of turf at the edge of the curb
   And everywhere greens. Your step
Quickens over graves leveled into bypath.

MIDDELBURG, ZEELAND

Can Zeeland have a *middel*, if its body's
compass dissolves at flood-tide? When the North
Sea sweeps eastwards, rooted coastal sod
melts into seaweed, and furrows in ploughed earth
trail off as wave troughs. There can be no heart-
land where salt fog bleaches the red from roses,
or where blood spilled when bombers found their target
has dried to clay in dark brick rebuilt houses.

Climb higher, to the ancient abbey's courtyard.
Here older blood, compounded with silt and sand
over long years, as marsh gave way to sward
and swamp to wood, rises from its nether land
to fountain up through this beech trunk: clay-grey barked,
and now the centre of a crimson-petalled circle.

THE TREE ON RUE DESCARTES

from the French of Yves Bonnefoy

Passerby,
Look at this tall tree and through it,
It will do.

Because the same scored, spattered street-tree
Is all nature, all heaven,
Here birds perch, here wind stirs, the sun
Here declares the same hope, in spite of death.

Philosopher,
If you chance to have this tree on your street
Your thoughts will be less burdened, your eyes more light,
Your hands more eager for less of night.

In the *Arabian Nights*, a fishless fisherman
fetches up a genie. We never learn what his wife
did while he was busy hauling in one of the sea's
bottled mysteries. Perhaps she was mending his nets
and trying to figure out ways to sauté water.
If they lived in Burano, she'd have been making lace

to make ends meet. A Burano woman's webs of lace
caught more hardy dinners than the eels her fisherman-
husband coaxed from the canals' beds of brackish water
on autumn tides. With her two feet on dry land, his wife
cast off, trawling for nothing but the spun linen nets
themselves, weavings legendary from the seven seas

to the deserts of Arabia. Of course the sea's
genius had magicked up all their prosperity. Lace
the waves threw on their shores was matrix both for the nets
that yielded scaled harvests up to landless fishermen
and for the finer, embroidered needlework their wives
sold when the fish weren't running. Living on water,

they took their living from it. And their deaths, when water
brought the islanders cargoes of plague from overseas.
Benumbed by the sea's unstoppered draught, many a wife
turned her needle from those wisp-thin filaments of lace
to coarse sailcloth, a broad-stitched shroud for her fisherman's
last setting-out. Yet, too fine to be caught in earth's nets,

Burano's lore lives on. Boat crews still construe the nets
of cross-currents that breezes weave across the water's
warp, before embarking with their fellow fishermen
for the day's haul while, more ethereal than the sea's
crystalline lattices, *punto in aria* lace
is conjured up by those who fish with needles. Are wives

and husbands the island's genies? A lacemaking wife
traps that most elusive fish, light, in her bone-white nets,
and light's other half, reflection, plays off the lacework
of scales in her other half's nets.   Yet this watery
place's most famous genius owed nothing to the sea –
one Baldassare Galuppi. Neither fisherman

nor wife, he cast on scored nets waves of sound lighter than
the scales of fish or man. Listen: your mind's eye will see
sunrise float on the lace-fringed carpet of the water.

TWO LONG-DISTANCE FLYERS

Both navigate currents the eye is blind to   whimbrel
by scaling cataracts of windstream   violinist
threading   through echolocation   corridors of soul.

Pinions   symmetrical and tapered   power her flight
but not that of her call   swept skyward on wings of breath
unseen except when mist ghost-writes it on morning air.

His wings   one wide one skinny   in an unpromising
collaboration of horsehair   wood   and steel   can't fly
but scraped together   raise song from black spots on
    black lines.

Plucked harpstring arpeggios fall from the wader's long
downsloped scimitar beak   like raindrops from a branch tip
to ripple in the ear-pools of her near whimbrel kin.

Wingstroke by wingstroke   the violinist dives back through
the downpour of years   fingering his way to the beat
of a composer's pulse   the flow of its allegro.

Beyond the eye's purview too   magnetic force that guides
the feathered warmth home to breeding grounds   the
    string and bow
arrowing notes to nest in a distant listener.

NOLI ME TANGERE

from the French of Yves Bonnefoy

A flake hovers in the renewed
blue, last flake of the big snow.

And it's as if she entered the garden, she
who dreamed what might be:
this look, this simple god, no recollection
of the tomb, no thought but happiness,
no future
but melting into the blue of the world.

"No, don't touch me," he would say,
even his nay-saying pure light.

asleep these three hundred years
under a green counterpane
of moss, wakens. No salt tears
brim the eye's *o*, autumn rain

beading it with mirror-gleam.
Why need his other eye, one
sighted in his carver's dream,
ever open if this stone

can hold so much light? Double
ring, concentric, no downward
Dante-whorl, blue untroubled
by retribution or cloud.

A partnership from the start,
hammerstone pecking birdshape
while kingfisher beak darted
into the grained sea. Fishers

both, and red-tree kin: the man
cedar-sheltered, the bird, perched
on peeling arbutus branch,
reaping waves aeons before

rafts surfaced with earth carvers
to plant this risen image,
sky-eyed, stone-winged survivor
of flesh, bone, and blue plumage.

ENCHANTMENTS*

They carry all their afters with them   and though sometimes
a single after weighs more than two of their battered
warped wood-framed suitcases   none makes any impact on

the airport scales   not the after of their whaling shrine's
removal   a hundred years back   to the museum
which leaves them still walking bent under the weight of loss

nor the after of their own removal from Yuquot
when the government closed their school   an after
    which you
might think cause enough to keep them off the
    plane   reeking

as it does of alcohol mixed with bitter discharge
from the pulp mill next to their new home   and of dead fish
tarnishing Gold River's waters   maybe the lightness

of their befores counterbalances the afters   up-
thrust of whales gamboling thick as party balloons be-
fore factory ships burst them with harpoon guns   doorposts

sending spirits up to the clouds before Captain Cook
came knocking with iron and disease   unpeopling them
with the name Nootka   then hollowing Yuquot's headland

trove of winds from the four quarters into the empty
skull of Friendly Cove   but now the elders bring those winds
with them to the museum as their voices unfold

enchantments packed alongside befores and afters   air
quick with sea-breath   with four thousand years of
    seal-calls   wails
of loons homing to one another   chatter-hubbub of winter
    wrens

sipping draughts spiced with cedar and seaweed   and the gold-
crowned sparrow's *see mee home see mee home*   their
    enchantments
like misty breezes embracing deeps and heights   caress

ancestral wooden figures   stroke the carved whales' grooved
    backs
and enter the vision-hallowed doorways of shamans'
· skulls   filling those coves once again with the light of song.

NOTES

"Placentia Island"

This poem is based on the experiences of the Kellams, Art (1911–1985) and Nan (1911–2001). Attempting to gain complete independence from both the post-traumatic stress and the materialism that followed World War II – when Art had worked at building bombers for Lockheed – they lived alone on Maine's Placentia Island for nearly forty years. Their isolation, originally sought as an end in itself, gradually became the means of developing a deeper awareness of their vital interdependence with the lives and cycles of the natural world. See Peter P. Blanchard, *We Were an Island* (University Press of New England, 2010).

"Paper Covers Rock"

The opening lines are taken from *Marlene Creates: Landworks 1979–1991* (Art Gallery, Memorial University of Newfoundland, 1993), where the nature photographer discusses her series of temporary landworks, *Paper, Stones and Water.*

"Polar Visions"

Captain John Ross aborted his 1818 attempt to find a northwest passage when he saw his access cut off by a chain of mountains – a vision discredited in 1819 when his former lieutenant Edward Parry sailed clear through the same inlet. However, in 1833 Ross was given a hero's welcome home after successfully guiding his crew through four winters of polar exploration. Captain Robert F. Scott's 1911–12 expedition to the South Pole – documented in his famous diaries and his recently discovered photographs of its crew and its boot-clad Manchurian ponies – ended in disaster.

"The Guide Speaks"

British-born Malcolm Miller has given remarkable guided tours of Chartres Cathedral for over fifty years. This poem attempts to capture his voice on one of those walks, as he leads visitors through the Cathedral that has become his second home.

"Enchantments"

Yuquot ("wind comes from all directions") was the site of the first European contact on the northwest coast, and became known by traders as Friendly Cove. The *cheesum* or whaler's shrine of the Mowachaht people there was bought in 1903 by the American Museum of Natural History in New York, where it still resides pending further negotiations. It contains 88 wooden figures, 4 carved whales, and 16 human skulls.

ACKNOWLEDGMENTS

Earlier versions of these poems, sometimes with different titles, appeared in *The Antigonish Review, Arc, Audeamus, The Fiddlehead, Grain, The Malahat Review*, the *Southwest Review*, the *University of Toronto Quarterly*, and in *Peter Cserháti – Hidden Treasures in Woodcarving, Sculpture, and Sketches: Ekphrastic Poems by John Reibetanz* (Toronto: Rufus Books, 2012), *Cry Uncle*, ed. Allan Briesmaster (Toronto: Aeolus House, 2013), and *Poems for an Anniversary*, ed. David Kent (Toronto: St. Thomas Poetry Series, 2013). My thanks go to all the editors for their continuing encouragement. I also want to thank Roo Borson, judge of the 2014 P.K. Page Founders' Award for Poetry at *The Malahat Review* for choosing "Fresco Magic."

I am grateful to Yves Bonnefoy and to Beverley Bie Brahic for their genial response to my translations of Bonnefoy's "Noli me tangere" (from *Début et fin de la neige*) and "L'Arbre de la rue Descartes" (from *La longe chaîne de l'ancre*), and to Geneviève Lebrun-Taugourdeau for arranging permissions at Mercure de France. I am also grateful to Petra Hardt at Suhrkamp Verlag and to Victoria Fox at Farrar, Straus and Giroux for permissions to publish my translations of Durs Grünbein's "Wieder vorm Telephon," "Unmöglich zu fliegen," and "Solange nach Gras sprieszt" (all part of "Variationen auf kein Thema," from *Falten und Fallen*) and "Club of Rome," from *Nach den Satiren*; Grünbein's originals have all been subsequently published in the dual-language *Ashes for Breakfast* (Farrar, Straus and Giroux, 2005).

Further encouragement and inspired suggestions have once more come from the Vic writing group, especially this time from Allan Briesmaster, Sue Chenette, Jeremy Harman, Maureen Hynes, Ruth Roach Pierson, and Leif Vaage. I have also been buoyed by the friendship, keen interest, and support of John Barton, Barry Dempster, Richard Greene, Ross Leckie, and Al Moritz, and blessed at McGill-Queen's by the enthusiastic and knowledgeable editorial attention of Allan Hepburn. As ever, my greatest debt is to my first critic, most keen-eyed and most kind, my wife Julie.